LETTERS TO ELLEN

Letters to Ellen

Gilbert Meilaender

WILLIAM B. EERDMANS PUBLISHING COMPANY
GRAND RAPIDS, MICHIGAN / CAMBRIDGE, U.K.

To Hannah and Ellen
individual pearls of equal price

© 1996 Wm. B. Eerdmans Publishing Co.
255 Jefferson Ave. S.E., Grand Rapids, Michigan 49503 /
P.O. Box 163, Cambridge CB3 9PU U.K.

Printed in the United States of America

01 00 99 98 97 96   7 6 5 4 3 2 1

ISBN 0-8028-4111-2

Contents

Preface

In the Fall of 1992 David Heim called me in search of material for *The Christian Century*. He wanted a series of short pieces about the Christian life — pieces written not in the style of a professional ethicist but as first-order reflection accessible to a general audience. After giving the idea some thought, and after another conversation with him, I chanced upon the approach that resulted in these letters. Not all the letters included here were first published in *Christian Century*, but the majority were.

Why letters from a mother to her daughter at college? It happened that one of my daughters had begun college only that year, so the idea suggested itself rather naturally. But for several reasons I needed somehow to distance myself from the letters. I wanted to remember that I was not writing — or, at least, not trying to write — treatises in "Christian ethics." I wanted some distance from my own life as a way of enabling me to pull into the letters ideas and events that had little basis in my personal experience. And, I must admit, I wanted to find some enjoyment in the project. It is harder work than one might imagine, and I needed to have some fun while doing it.

Hence, letters from a mother to her daughter. Though no doubt a stretch in some ways, it didn't seem as if it should be impossible. After all, I have been getting advice from my own mother for many years. (It is a process, I have discovered, that has no natural stopping point — except, I guess, death.) And, in addition, for many years I have also been listening to my wife offer counsel to our two sons and two daughters. I hope I have learned something from listening to these two women whom I regard as wise. Indeed, on at least a few occasions in the letters I know that I have been little more than a conduit for advice I first heard from them.

At the same time I have drawn freely from my own experience, my reading, people I know, and conversations of many sorts. All of that, however, has been refracted through the prism of imagination in such a way that these are not simply my letters to my daughter. Some things in the letters reflect directly our personal experience; others are entirely fictional. Still others transmute into one form or another people whom I have known over many years and in different places. It will do little good to try to identify them (as the members of my family have tried), since in some cases I can't do it myself.

The letters are meant to be serious, not chatty. I suppose few parents would write such letters any more to their children, but, then, ours is an impoverished world in many ways. Although the letters are meant to be serious, I must repeat that for me seriousness of purpose does not always require a serious tone. Attempting to enjoy myself along the way, I could not resist a few inside jokes. Any reader who takes these letters literally enough to suppose, for example, that Ellen's Mom was not really happy until she met me will, I regret to say, be far from the truth. A reader who thought the real Ellen loved to rake leaves would be surprised to get to know her. (She does, however, throw the remote control.) And a reader who supposes that the father in this family constantly wants to acquire new and better tools is welcome to check my badly bent handsaw and listen to stories of my ineptitude. Such moments in the letters give my children opportunity to say what they like best: "Right, Dad."

About the content of the letters themselves there should be little need here for comment from me. For the most part they discuss the ordinary and everyday, not large questions of public concern (although one might, of course, place Michael Jordan's retirement into that category). When writing them I often had in mind the Decalog, to which Christians have regularly turned when thinking about the contours of the moral life. Many aspects of the Decalog are treated — the sabbath, marriage, our attitude toward possessions and property, loving God above all else. But it was not my only pattern. One might also consider how many virtues receive attention in the letters — contentment, fidelity, gratitude, authenticity, humility, hope, simplicity, trust, even studiousness. A few very large topics of importance for Christian life — prayer, miracles, death, vocation — are also discussed, even if in necessarily brief fashion.

On the whole, the letters are not meant to provide arguments to those who are not Christians. They are not intended to offend, though they are surely opinionated in many places. They aim to think about what it means to live as a Christian, and I only wish it had not taken a call from David Heim to move me to write them for my children.

Rising to the Occasion

Dear Ellen:

I want to try to write to you regularly while you're at college. In part it's because, as you wrote in your letter, checking for mail is an important part of the day — especially if you get some. In fact, when you wrote that, it reminded me that the best reason to have a job is that it gives a person two chances each day to get some mail. Most of it is junk, of course, but checking it is always an occasion for hope. No doubt I'll write you with news on occasion, but I also want to write now and then about what it means to live as a Christian. Perhaps I can entice you into writing back.

Recently you set me to thinking when you recounted what had been said at your dorm meeting about the "informal" understanding governing the presence of men in women's rooms (especially overnight). I recounted it with dismay (though without surprise) to Mr. Hollander, but he took quite a different view. "Look," he said, "college students are at an age when their hormones are raging. But they're far too young to marry. Indeed, they don't yet know who they are, and the formation of that self is what college is about. So of course we have to recognize that sexual activity apart from commitment (much less marriage)

1

will be common. But it's far better than rushing them into marriage before they're fully formed."

And suddenly I realized why I believe in early marriage. (Relax. Not all that early. It's fine if you wait a few years.) What a false understanding of life this is — and what a mistaken picture of the place of marriage in life. The point of marriage is that self-formation becomes a joint venture. I do not form myself. I am formed by another to whom I have given myself — another whom I love, yet who will prove to be strangely different and resistant.

This strikes me now as an illustration of a much more wide-ranging principle. The covenant of marriage is just that — a covenant. It cuts deeply into our personal identity. It takes time and history seriously as the matrix in which we are formed and within which we must learn to be faithful. It accepts the fact that along the way we may often encounter what is unexpected and, indeed, could never have been planned or predicted. A seriously ill husband. A disabling accident. A lost job. A child. "Let it be to me according to your word," Mary said, when her plans were rudely interrupted. The Christian life is supposed to be in large part learning to rise to the occasion, to accept the unexpected.

This is because Christians take time seriously. How could we not since God has entered it? If we suppose we must be fully formed before we marry, what can be the significance of the marriage covenant? Only self-fulfillment, I suspect. Two people, knowing who they are and will be, come together for their mutual satisfaction. I don't mean to underestimate the happiness that may bring to people, but it's not the point of marriage for Christians. For us marriage should be an arena in which we are formed over time — in unpredictable and sometimes unwanted ways. We don't stand outside the flow of time as if we could say for sure who we are and what we will be. We stand together within time, with only the image of God's faithfulness to guide us, and then we enter a covenant in which God will begin to reshape us in that image.

The rejection of time seems to me a characteristic of our age. We've lost the sense of life as a story in which we are characters — in which the idea is to play our part well, not to suppose that we are the author. This shows itself in lots of ways; maybe I'll write about some of them another time. One result is clear: we have lost our appreciation for the virtue of fidelity. But you should remember that we cannot give ourselves wholly unless we include the future. Try out that idea at the next dorm meeting.

Love,
Mom

Taking Pains

Dear Ellen:

I thought that by starting with sex I might get an answer out of you, but perhaps I took too philosophical a turn with all that business about taking time seriously. At any rate, that's what your father said when he read it.

Let's consider something you really do care about: Michael Jordan. Remember how devastated you were when the news broke that he was retiring? Dad called you from New York when he was on a trip there. He said he knew you'd need some consolation. And Paul called you too, just to make sure you'd heard the news. My reaction was: "Well, at least she may stop throwing the remote control across the room when the Bulls aren't winning."

You know I'm not much of a fan, but I do have a theory about what made Jordan so compelling to watch. I don't think it was just the glitter of his style, though, of course, even I could see that he did incredible things. I think it was the fact that he didn't just rely on all that natural talent. There was a perfectionist quality to him, the attitude of a craftsman. And I think that is what you were responding to in him — especially as you became an increasingly knowledgeable fan. He communicated the sense

5

that he cared about how the game was played — and wanted it done right.

People like that are always compelling, and I think they see something very important about life. I'm less and less drawn to well-rounded people, more and more attracted to those who do something — almost anything — with care. And it doesn't much matter what it is that so commands our energy and attention. It may be basketball. It may be writing. It may be raising some children. It may be managing an office. To engage our powers as best we can in some task — that should be the goal. And for the rest we can quote Chesterton: "If a thing is worth doing, it is worth doing badly." It's true, of course, that some callings — such as being a mother — demand the skills of a generalist. But there still must be a central core to our concern if we are to have a center ourself. You know I never worried much whether the house was neat. But I paid a lot of attention to you. Took pains over you, if I may put it that way.

In the last few years I've come to apply the same principle to the academic life. I've ceased to believe much in those endless distribution requirements that universities are reinstituting. College students study far too many subjects these days. What I'd like for you to do is learn a few things — take pains over them and learn them well. (Your father suggests that some subjects may be too insubstantial to warrant such single-minded devotion. But if he's right, as he may be, people will come to see that they're not worth the full engagement of our emotional and intellectual powers.)

Why should we all want to be the same sort of well-rounded people? Why should husbands and wives want to be mirror images of each other, dutifully splitting every chore down the middle? Stones laid in a row, as C. S. Lewis said, are less beautiful than an arch. In a choir — and, I dare to believe, in

6

the heavenly choir — we will sing parts. The idea is not to sing every part equally well, but to harmonize.

And there's the point I've been leading up to: Michael Jordan, magnificent as he was, needed Bill Cartwright (and even — especially on those occasions when you were throwing the remote — Will Perdue). To deny this, to deny that we must each find our own calling and devote ourself to it, to imagine that we should all be alike . . . all that is really a flight from harmony, from the inner meaning of a shared life. This is what the commandment against coveting is actually about. I must learn that in wanting to be the person you are, I blot out the person I am called to be. Find something you care about and devote yourself to it with a whole heart. Think of it as preparation for heaven.

Love,
Mom

Being Contented

Dear Ellen:

Of course you're right that when I said you should find something you care about and devote yourself to it with a whole heart, I didn't mean you had to do just one thing your entire life. As Rousseau said, my ideas are all consistent, but I can't say them all at once! I've also said that we must learn to think of ourselves as characters in a story Someone else is writing. Your role may change as the story develops, but in any moment you must find it and play it as best you can. And be content to do so.

Contentment is not a virtue much praised these days. When Mrs. Houston, in her perceptive if rambling sort of way, said something at last Sunday's Bible class about the importance of contentment, three people jumped down her throat. They saw praise for contentment as a way of trying to keep people from bettering their lot in life or seeking simple justice. And, of course, I'm sure it's true that contentment has often been praised by the rich when speaking to the poor.

But I have in mind a different way in which contentment seems almost essential for living well. Don't you get the feeling that nearly everyone you meet has the same ideal — to be about

30 years old, at the peak of their powers, healthy, and in control of their life? It's as if there is one ideal moment in life and all would be well if we could just freeze the action right at that point. Not that many years ago you had a fit because we said you couldn't go to a sixth-grade prom. You thought that what was good for the high school kids was good for you. We, to your dismay, thought that being in sixth grade and being in 11th grade were quite different chapters in the story of your life. (And even you thought it ridiculous that some of the sixth graders arrived at the prom in limos.)

Is it any wonder that turning 40 becomes a crisis for so many people? Or that women who are clearly senior citizens traipse around malls in stretch pants? (You and Carrie were sitting in your room laughing about that just the last time we visited you, but, of course, you are still young.) Or is it a surprise that every sports team David plays on must be dressed up like professionals and end its season with a long tournament — just like the older boys?

Just the other day I was thinking about how you and I used to rake leaves together in the fall. Somehow you always seemed more susceptible to the splendors of autumn than Paul or Hope. (The jury's still out on David). The leaves really are splendid, but you can't hang on to their beauty. They have to fall, so that we can have winter — which, after all, has its own beauty, though you have not yet learned to appreciate it as you ought.

People love to quote Ecclesiastes: "For everything there is a season." But we don't live as if we believe it, as if there were stages in life to be passed through (each of them, as something I read put it, equidistant from God). And then the professor in your government class wonders how we are to get a grip on health care expenditures. I can't imagine that we will ever manage that unless we learn to cultivate the virtue of contentment —

which frees us from forever wanting to exist in just one stage of life. (Think how dull a story that would be.)

So relish the moment in life that you've been given. When assignments pile up and you'd rather be a little girl again, don't be too nostalgic for the past. And don't be ridden by dreams of the future — which may never materialize. Think of these few years as a gift you have been given. (Not just from us. Thank your scholarship as well.) Never again will you be set free just to read and think. Don't act like a child. But appreciate the fact that others are bearing responsibilities that set you free. And I would not be your mother if I did not add in closing: don't act as if you were married before you are. For everything there is a season.

Love,
Mom

Loving God with the Mind

Dear Ellen:

You're right. The advice I gave in my last letter is different from what your president said at that beginning-of-year convocation we attended with you. I wrote: "Never again will you be set free just to read and think." Your president said: "Don't think you are here simply to study. You are here also to serve, and the college is organizing community service opportunities to enable that."

I'm sure you hoped, by recalling this, to get me to rise to the bait, and you have succeeded. I thought it a peculiar comment from a college president. Would he like to be reminded how much it calls to mind the rhetoric of fraternities? At any rate, I admit to a good bit of suspicion about such community service emphases. In the first place, it's an emphasis many students are all too eager to embrace. Academic work is hard and often grueling. Only people who've never seriously attempted it think otherwise. It's hard work to get a problem right when you just can't seem to crack its secret. When you've drafted a paper and realize that it isn't yet very good — and that you could make it much better by starting over — it's hard to commit yourself to the work a better paper would require. Going down to the soup kitchen and working there instead gives us a good reason to succumb to the temptation to turn in second-rate work.

But the issue goes deeper than this alone. For now, I think, your calling is to be a student, as good a student as you can be. I don't mean, of course, that you must become a great scholar. And I don't mean that you should do nothing but study. Maybe you'll find some time to spend at the soup kitchen. Nevertheless, for these few years of your life your primary calling is an academic one.

You must learn to love God not just with the heart, but also with the mind. Do you remember the hymn "Take My Life and Let It Be"? I once knew a pastor who said he would not allow his congregation to sing the fourth stanza of that hymn. It's the stanza that begins: "Take my silver and my gold, / Not a mite would I withhold." He claimed they couldn't sing it honestly and therefore shouldn't sing it at all.

I suspect, though, that we have every bit as much trouble living out the next lines of the same stanza: "Take my intellect and use / Every power as thou shalt choose." As I said, this doesn't mean that you must aim at becoming a great scholar. Nor does it mean that you won't sometimes have to admit that you simply don't know an answer you'd like to know. And certainly it doesn't mean that you should take pride in the right answers when you do get them, since the light by which you see is not one that you generate yourself.

God is light. That metaphor has to do with the mind, seeing with the eye of the mind in a creation bathed in the light of God. Thus we are enabled and invited to pursue knowledge into the dark corners of our world. Not just "spiritual" knowledge either. How to use a semicolon. How flowers are nourished and reproduce. What makes Jane Austen a great writer. What we mean when we speak of justice. How to decline the Latin verb.

Love God with the mind, Jesus says. Not just with your hands and feet, not just with your voice and will. But with your powers of understanding, deepened and sharpened. When you were baptized, you received the sign of the cross upon "the forehead and the breast" — that is, upon mind and heart. You should, therefore, never be able to imagine that the life of the mind is not serious business for you.

Remember the little poem they used in Sunday school to teach you how to make the sign of the cross, recalling your baptism: "God be in my head . . . God be in my heart . . . God be on the left of me . . . God be on the right of me." Obviously, the heart counts. But for the moment I want to encourage you to use the years of college you've been given to learn to love God with the mind.

Love,
Mom

Uncompulsive

Dear Ellen:

So you feel that your life is too rushed — too frantic and hectic? I will not say what your father would: "Why, these are the easiest years of your life. We're paying lots of money so you can live utterly free of responsibility!" There's a grain of truth in what he says, but I want to offer a very different suggestion.

If you want to be less rushed and frantic, stop doing any of your work on Sunday. I know that sounds crazy, since you say there's not enough time as it is to get work done. But perhaps what you need is a reminder that the work isn't just yours — that we can call nothing simply "ours." Not even our time. You need to learn again what you surely know intellectually — that life is a trust from God and must be lived in trust.

I first came to understand this by reading Karl Barth. I had to read volume III/4 of *Church Dogmatics.* It is a very long book. But good.

I began reading it because I had to, and I was quite busy at the time with other things. I had no idea what the volume would be about; I knew only that this was supposed to be Barth's "special ethics," in which he would, no doubt, take up "important" moral problems. And, of course, when I thought about important moral problems I had in mind the sorts of issues Carrie studied in philosophy last semester: warfare, abortion, euthanasia, animal rights. You know what the list looks like.

I sat down one morning to read — busy, but ready to see the greatest theologian of the twentieth century tackling some weighty moral problems. And I was stunned to realize that the first issue Barth chose to discuss was "the holy day." This great theologian, writing on big questions, began with how Christians ought to keep the holy day holy — by, to put it a little too simply, refraining from work, giving themselves to the praise of God, and spending time with their neighbors.

I was, as I say, stunned. But also liberated. I think it's the closest I've ever came to having a "religious experience." And as best I can, I haven't worked on Sunday since then. By which I mean: I haven't done things I thought I had to do. I have tried to remember that the holy day exists to set me free from compulsion — free to trust God to care for me. And to the degree I manage it on that day, I think I'm more likely to manage it on the other days of the week.

I have gradually come to see that the implications of this extend far beyond the busyness of my life or yours. Remember those talks you and Carrie had when she was writing her paper on environmental ethics? It was all about our obligations to future generations. That's all well and good, but I don't see how we can really hope to care for the earth until we develop virtues like gratitude, trust, and contentment. And aren't those precisely the virtues we are cultivating when we stop doing what we *have* to do for a day and thank God for his care? Let me know what you think.

Love,
Mom

Morning and Evening

Dear Ellen:

Don't feel guilty just because you haven't found any regular pattern for your prayers and devotions. The fact that it concerns you is a good indication that you're taking it seriously. And the truth is that being regular about prayer is one of the hardest things to accomplish.

You may be trying to do too much — and, therefore, inevitably ending up doing too little. Short readings are best. I've often decided to use a book for my devotions, but then I find myself unable to break it into readable sections, and pretty soon I'm backsliding again. Of course, there are books whose sections are short enough to be manageable — *Screwtape Letters* comes to mind as a nice example. You need selections short enough to read and think about.

That's why, wholly apart from its unique position in Christian faith, the Bible works so well. You can take it in little bits and pieces. Even so, of course, some parts work better than others. I wouldn't start with Leviticus, if I were you. Christians have always used the Psalms this way, and, if you do, you will quickly develop your own favorites — psalms that seem to speak to your condition. And you will be led back to others that hadn't been favorites when your circumstances change. Hymns also work well — reading just one at a time and pondering it.

Prayers are even harder. I find it almost impossible to say even the shortest of prayers with complete concentration, don't you? Since the One to whom we pray is not immediately apparent, we fill that emptiness with something else. I don't think you can overcome this just by concentrating harder. If your experience is anything like mine, you'll find yourself realizing that — once again — your mind has been wandering. The trick, I think, is simply to offer that wandering thought to God — make it part of your prayer — and carry on. After all, the idea isn't to concentrate on yourself. Too much effort here is self-defeating.

I myself like fixed forms of prayer. I like to read prayers aloud. In part that's because I find my mind wanders less under those circumstances. And in part it's because such prayers are likely to incorporate a wider scope of needs and concerns than would naturally occur to me. John Baillie's *A Diary of Private Prayer* is the very best. It's old, of course, and it never attempts to be cute or folksy. Fine with me. I like a little formality when stepping into the presence of the Almighty. An added benefit is that Baillie's prayers are beautifully crafted. They'll initiate you into a cadence of speech that the average sermon has long since lost. I know you have the book. We gave it to you for Christmas a couple years ago. Try it.

You may have to experiment with different times of day to discover what works best for you. Although not everyone agrees, I still like morning and evening best for our private devotions. To take up the day as God's gift and offer it back to him at day's end brackets the days of our life in a way that will take on added meaning for you over the years. As the hymn puts it: "To you our morning hymns ascended / Your praise shall hallow now our rest."

Then, when you find that you've gone a pretty long stretch without being faithful in your devotions, remember that you are part of a body of believers. They have been praying for you and on your behalf. They have been saying "*Our* Father" — including you, at your most faithless, in their prayers. When on occasion I wake in the middle of the night and my mind begins to work, I like to recall that somewhere some Cistercians are praying for all of us — and not just for us, but with us in the Body. And more generally, while I sleep Christians elsewhere are rising to offer the church's petitions and praise — for me and with me.

The hymn gets it right: "The sun, here having set, is waking / Your children under western skies, / And hour by hour, as day is breaking, / Fresh hymns of thankful praise arise." Join in when you can.

Love,
Mom

Being Held Responsible

Dear Ellen:

The rumor you heard is true. Pastor Preis really did run off with the church secretary. I know it sounds like a bad soap opera, but the people at the Methodist Church have been badly shaken. After all, he had been there 17 years — long enough to enter deeply into people's lives. I, too, feel sorry for the family. And the issue is larger than the hurt they personally have suffered. The church more generally — not just this one family, not even this one congregation — suffers immeasurably from such incidents.

When I said as much to Pastor Haden, though, he wasn't ready to agree, "Judge not," he said. "The church always describes itself as a community of sinners, so why should this surprise us?" Then he suggested that I might be making the common mistake of holding the clergy to a higher standard than I expected from others.

To which I said, "You bet I hold you to a higher standard. Like it or not, your capacity to harm the faith and the faithful is very great, and you'd better take that fact seriously." As you can imagine, he wasn't too pleased. The conversation set me to thinking about the relation between what we say and what we do. When I was about your age, we always used to sing "They'll Know We Are Christians by Our Love." When I got a little older I realized that the theology of that song is rather suspect. Theologically, we can't depend on our behavior to validate the word about Jesus, since, of course, our behavior has its ups and downs. And logically it's quite true that the validity of a statement depends only on the reasons given in support of it. That a scoundrel offers the reasons is irrelevant — if they're good reasons. And, of course, if moral advice and admonition could be offered only by the righteous, there wouldn't be any such advice.

But logic alone does not determine our views. I have found it very difficult to take seriously the thought of one whose actions don't seem to fit his ideas. I remember the effect it had on me when I learned a little about Tillich's life. In politics, alas, the examples are legion. Closer to home there was Mrs. Hurley. Everybody thought she was the best principal they'd known until the news came out about what she'd done to her own children. In lots of ways she still was a good principal, but it was impossible to think of her in the same way.

Now that I've started writing about this, I realize what deep waters these are. Isn't this the problem every parent faces? We must try to teach our children well, must set before them high ideals and lofty aspirations. But to the degree that we succeed in this task, we train people who will one day find us wanting. If they find us too wanting, if our behavior doesn't seem to fit our teaching, we may destroy everything we've worked to build. I tried a few years ago to get you to read *The Duke of Deception.* Maybe you should try again. I remember vividly how terrifying I found that story of the boy gradually realizing that his father (whom he loved!) was a con man, the duke of deception. And it was terrifying because, at some level, so are we all.

Shall we, then, never judge? No. Sinful as we are, we can still say that Pastor Preis's sin has brought harm to many people. For that he is responsible, and we need to hold him to such responsibility.

And what of our parents — who are all, at the deepest level, less than they pretend to be? They, too, bear an awesome responsibility. When they fall short of the ideals they have taught, we cannot say that such failure is harmless. But gently, Ellen, gently.

Love,
Mom

Christmas for the World

Dear Ellen:

As I sit at my desk looking out the window, we are getting the first real snow of the winter. As always, it is lovely. And in less than two weeks, you'll be home for Christmas.

I have already set aside two days when you and I can go shopping and your father is free to meet David after school. Bring your walking shoes. Those will be long days.

Of course, according to Pastor Haden's sermon yesterday, you and I are part of the problem of Christmas. I don't understand why contentedly bourgeois clergy feel so compelled to work off their radical impulses right before Christmas. He made all the standard points: A Christian holy day turned into a commercial success. Shoppers and party-goers worn out before the day actually arrives. Cards sent out of nothing more than a sense of obligation. And all that work — cookies to bake, carols to sing, lights to string, Christmas specials on TV to watch.

I'll say this for him, though. He did it all rather catchily. The innkeeper in Bethlehem is, he said, the symbol for how we celebrate Christmas. All he knew was that lots of people were coming. That meant work — rooms to be cleaned, food to be prepared and served, and, perhaps, a little profit to be made. But then he missed the chance of a lifetime: Jesus wasn't born in his inn.

As I say, I enjoyed the performance greatly, but I don't suppose that's the way one ought to respond to a sermon. You know, though, it's not really very radical to be cynical about Christmas cards (and letters) or to take potshots at businesses. Despite all the fireworks, I'm afraid Pastor Haden missed the point.

Which is incarnation. God comes to the world, taking human life into his own life. There is a way of celebrating Christmas which can — with the best of intentions — miss that. As if we need to worry that the world might find a way to be happy all on its own.

God comes to a world that needs him and that, wittingly or not, seeks him. Why do merchants make good profits at Christmas? In part, perhaps, because buried deep within us is a desire to give to others. It's a desire we usually manage to stifle, but at Christmas it breaks through and overcomes even the worst of us. Why do we keep on sending those cards? Because we have not lost entirely the sense that we are created for life with each other.

I'm sure you remember the Advent hymn by John Bowring in which the traveler and the watchman carry on a little dialogue. "Watchman," says the traveler, "tell us of the night, what its signs of promise are." For me, at least, that is the secret question of the world. Stifled so much of the year, it breaks forth at Christmas.

We could not stand the selfishness and greed if there were not this time when even the Scrooges among us become transformed by the spirit of Christmas (or is that the Spirit of Christmas?). We could not stand the darkness that is all around us were there not this time when brightly colored lights shine through that darkness. We should not despise the world's celebration of Christmas or grow cynical about it.

We should join in. Christmas carols, tired feet, long hours spent shopping, lights and decorations, festive foods, songs about the Christmas we used to know. Christmas ought not be too sterile or antiseptic an occasion. It is for the world, because in the incarnate Son God is for the world. Of course we do more than just join in. When the traveler asks for signs of the coming dawn, the watchman's task is not to deplore the question. It is to answer: "Traveler, darkness takes its flight; doubt and terror are withdrawn."

I wish Pastor Haden would take to heart the second lesson read in our service yesterday. "Be patient, therefore, brethren, until the coming of the Lord." Be patient with the world — as, in fact, God is.

Love,
Mom

Plunging In

Dear Ellen:

I'm sorry I wasn't home when you called with questions about your research paper. The difficulty you're experiencing is a very profound one. I've often puzzled over it.

Think about your assignment and why you're having trouble. You have to pick a topic for a paper on either the *Iliad* or the *Odyssey*, turn that topic in to your prof, and get started doing research — all of this before you've read either epic. I have to admit that I've given assignments like this one, but I've never been sure that I could, if pressed, offer a convincing explanation of how this "learning experience" is supposed to work. I suppose I would simply say that one has to plunge in. By plunging into water that's a little over your head, you learn to swim. Gradually you find your way around in the material, perhaps even "master" a little of it. I would say, though, that the prof owes you a bit more guidance — some possible topics, some important secondary sources, that sort of thing.

What you're experiencing is a little taste of the deepest mysteries of Christian living. When you were baptized you were, in a sense, given an assignment: to make the whole of your life a research paper in which you explore the meaning of trusting

31

God and try to draw the scattered threads of that life into a coherent whole that truly follows Jesus.

No one can just give you that ready-made. I'd like to, of course. So would your father. It's the temptation every parent faces. But when we brought you to baptism we were really recognizing that the Christian life is not our possession that you automatically inherit. We had to hand you over to God and pray for you. As we still do.

For years I've been puzzled about the attitude many people appear to have toward baptism. Even if they don't seem to care all that much about the church, they still bring their new little son or daughter to be baptized. They seem to think of baptism as a natural result of their connection to this little baby. Since they were once baptized, their child should be too.

But isn't the truth of baptism just the opposite of affirming a human connection? Being baptized is being handed over to God. The first thing to say about it, therefore, is that it is a deeply individualizing act. Having been baptized, that little child sets out on a journey in which she must learn to love Jesus more than father or mother. She is plunged into the waters of baptism, in which she must learn to swim.

You see what this means? Much as I often hate to admit it, you are writing your paper, not mine. And in writing the paper that is your life, plagiarism is not so much wrong as impossible. I cannot turn you into a Christian; only God can do that.

Still, you are not on this journey alone. If baptism is first an individualizing act, it also brings you into the community of the church. You become part of a "research group" that offers you guidance about topics that deserve your attention and sources that will repay your study. And even though I handed you over when I brought you for baptism, I am still joined with you in the community of the baptized, and I pray for you, my research partner.

Meanwhile, why not look closely at the scene in Book VI of the *Iliad* where Andromache begs Hector not to fight? You'll find more than one paper waiting to be written there. Or read Simone Weil's essay on the *Iliad*. You won't soon forget it.

Love,
Mom

Negative about Affirmation

Dear Ellen:

I finally managed to follow your recommendation and watch Stuart Smalley's "Daily Affirmation" on *Saturday Night Live.* It's every bit as funny as you said. Perhaps it ought to be required viewing for every church member. In fact, I've been thinking of suggesting to Pastor Haden that we all take a vow not to use the word "affirm" for a year. If we had to get along without the term, we might learn to think more clearly.

Whenever I start thinking this way, Mr. Hollander comes to mind. He's certainly a decent man, and I imagine he's a fine counselor, but sometimes he acts as if the whole of life were a counseling session. Your father says outrageous things just to bait him. Last week, for example, he suggested that we devise a method for publicly shaming high school students who had children. I was afraid Mr. Hollander might have a stroke.

But the point is serious. Hope and I started talking about it when she came home from a basketball game the other day. She tells me that everybody's excited when one of the girls brings her baby to a high school event. I can understand that. I can't think of anything more thrilling than a baby. But, then, how are we to put forward certain ideals about what marriage or a family should be? If we're so busy "affirming" these young girls and boys with their babies, we lose the capacity to distinguish right from wrong, the ideal from the flawed.

Why should we be surprised that the point of life for so many students becomes self-fulfillment? We have never suggested that they might have to make sacrifices in the name of an ideal. We don't hold them to anything, and, not surprisingly, pretty soon they don't hold themselves to any standards.

Just last week I went to a meeting of parents who wanted to discuss concerns about the high school. To my amazement, the constant refrain was that the teachers "just don't understand and appreciate" our children, and don't try to develop their talents enough. I sat quietly for as long as I could and then said that the real problem with the high school was that it didn't teach Latin. The nice thing about it was that they were conducting the meeting in a way intended to "affirm" all suggestions. Every comment was entered on a big chart at the front of the room. So my suggestion, too, will be transmitted to the school authorities.

Mr. Hollander says that someone with my training should understand that Christians, at least, should be people for whom forgiveness is front and center — which, of course, he equates with constant affirmation. But I'm not persuaded. Genuine forgiveness never paralyzes the capacity for moral judgment, since it forgives what is acknowledged as wrong and repented. That's a far cry from the affirmation talk that is clogging so many Christian arteries.

Moreover, there's a hidden element of condescension in much of that talk. If I try to hold you to an ideal, I don't simply "impose" my standards on you. I ask of you what I first ask of myself. That's the nature of an ideal: we hold it up not just for others but for ourselves. We don't distinguish ourselves from others. But when I simply affirm you without holding you to such ideals, I don't really take you seriously. And I make it too easy on myself. It's not particularly hard or costly for me to be affirming. What's hard, what requires a great deal of Christian virtue and ordinary tact, is caring about you while still holding you to an ideal. The hardest thing in the world is to fail a student while demonstrating concern for his or her well-being. The easiest thing in the world is to fudge the grade a little and pass that student.

It's the latter that's happening with all this "affirmation" talk — and I hereby renounce it for a year. If you will join the movement, we can declare ourselves its co-directors.

Love,
Mom

The Beginning of Wisdom

Dear Ellen:

You suggest that I overlooked something important in my perhaps too quick indictment of your peers. And you're right to
note that in sports they do have ideals and standards. (Not all
of them, of course. Don't forget noncompetitive Frisbee.) And
they often do manage to accept and comfort losers without
simply pretending that it doesn't matter who won or lost. In any
case, I grant your point.

You also asked a question that deserves a response: How
can we be so certain of the rightness of our ideals — for in-
stance, the ideals about marriage and family that I just assumed
in that last letter? Wouldn't a little humility be in order here,
since, after all, these are matters on which intelligent people often
disagree?

Leaving aside some of the larger philosophical problems,
don't you think Christians may have at least a partial answer to
the questions you raise? "The fear of the Lord is the beginning
of wisdom," the sage says. Take that verse seriously and you
will gain some confidence in our ability to know the truth about
how we ought to live, and you will also find the source of true
humility.

39

The fear of the Lord is the beginning of *wisdom.* For all its complexity and confusion, the world is not sheer chaos. It is creation. At its source lies the wisdom and understanding of God. Our lives are ordered toward community with God and each other. So there is order to be discerned, truth to be learned about what human beings need to be and ought to do.

Of course, we don't always see this truth rightly — and we often disagree about what we need to be and ought to do. We would see more truly if we feared and loved God more fully. Much of the time we don't really want a world in which the truth about how we ought to live could be learned. For such a world would sometimes — perhaps often — resist our projects and desires.

The simple fact that we often disagree about how to live needn't intimidate us into supposing that we can know nothing about such matters. For the world remains God's creation. In and through it God draws us — and sometimes tugs and pulls us — toward community. If others dispute your ideals, you must take them seriously and listen carefully. But most of all you must seek again that fear of the Lord that is the beginning of wisdom.

And do not forget that it is the *beginning* of wisdom. Because the divine light shines into our world we are able to see. We can look at things *in* that light and achieve some understanding. But we cannot look *at* the light itself, as if to lay hands on the Mystery. Our knowledge always remains incomplete, a beginning and a part of the truth, but no more. Shouldn't that give rise to a little humility?

Just don't think of humility as weak, as if it were a virtue for the intimidated. Remember Puddleglum, your favorite character in the Narnia stories. When the witch almost has him (and Jill and Eustace) believing that Aslan is only a dream, he holds fast to his ideal. "I'm on Aslan's side even if there isn't any Aslan to lead it. I'm going to live as like a Narnian as I can even if there isn't any Narnia."

That alone is not sufficient, of course, but it captures some of the power of an ideal. And by clinging to his ideal, Puddleglum did see a part of the truth. He was given genuine insight.

God will one day deepen and enrich that insight. In the meantime, you can work on the matter of "fearing the Lord," earnestly desiring the light. It will never hurt to begin your studies on your knees. You may see further from there.

Love,
Mom

Lenten Discipline

Dear Ellen:

It sounds as if your Ash Wednesday service was quite moving. I wish we could have been there for it, though ours wasn't bad either. It's probably terrible, but I have to admit that I "like" Lent better than Easter. I find that I almost never enjoy an Easter service. Somehow our attempts at festivity always seem inadequate to capture the meaning of Easter. Then, too, all those people come who can't or won't participate in the liturgy and who simply won't sing hymns. I remind myself, of course, that their presence testifies to some longing that has not yet been quenched — and that's a good thing.

Still, I like Lent, though it was a much bigger deal in our congregations when I was young than it is now. I like the hymns. I like the sense of progression the season gives. I like hearing again the passion narrative (even though the clergy often seem embarrassed by the simplicity of such an approach). And I like the invitation to discipline.

You say that you and your friends have decided to "add something" for Lent instead of "giving up" something. That's become quite common, I guess, and I don't suppose there's anything wrong with it. Still, I prefer to give up something. That comes a little closer to our true need, I suspect.

If I add something for Lent, I am tempted to think that all has been well with me — though, of course, there's always more good to be done in the world. So I do a little more of it for six weeks, and then I return to being the person with whom I was already reasonably well satisfied.

But to give up something — even something perfectly good in itself — is a lesson in how eagerly I tie my heart to passing goods, how easily I forget that every good thing comes from God and should lead me back to the one from whom it comes. We are fragile beings, easily enslaved. Giving up something reminds me that the grace of God actually can do something in me and to me. It doesn't, I find, tempt me to suppose that I'm really doing pretty well as is.

More important still is that "giving up" seems more like following Jesus on his way to the cross. Lent directs us to Jesus and invites us to draw nearer to him. Renunciation, so central to his story, seems an appropriate way to draw near. It makes clear that I am not just attempting to work on myself — to become a little better person than I have been. Rather, I am attempting to stand in the shade of Jesus' great act of renunciation. I am seeking to let him do for me what I cannot, in fact, do myself.

Remember two years ago when your father gave up Coke for Lent? None of us thought he could do it — there being few people who drink it for three meals a day and in the middle of the night as well. But he did, and, having done it, I'm confident he could do it again if it were asked of him. More important, it made that Lent a truly memorable exercise in renunciation for him.

To tell you the truth, buried in all this talk of adding something instead of giving up something I sometimes hear the faint vestiges of lingering anti-Catholicism among us Protestants. To be sure, we do not want to do what the Reformers would have called manufacturing "works," while at the same time we are failing to heed the most straightforward of commandments. But adding some new worthwhile task is more likely to tempt us in that direction. Better, I think, to relinquish for a time some good thing to which our heart clings tightly.

I see it simply as practice in following Jesus. Who can say what may one day be asked of us, how our discipleship may be tested? To have drawn closer to Jesus, and especially to his act of renunciation, is probably the best preparation there is. In countless ways our world is not particularly receptive to Christian faith. I often suspect that increasing renunciation will be asked of Christians within your lifetime. I do not say we should seek a cross; we can let it find us if it must. But I do say that we should seek to draw near to Jesus on his way to the cross and begin thereby to learn the meaning of renunciation.

Love,
Mom

Why Miracles Are Rare

Dear Ellen:

I spent some time thinking about your conversation with Jean. Her view that Christians should expect God to perform miracles in their lives isn't really all that uncommon, I suspect. At least not for a certain brand of Christian. And, as you realized, if that's not your brand, you may be uncertain how to respond. It might seem as if a believer ought to agree.

But you need to think about what it would actually mean to expect God regularly to perform miracles in our lives. What kind of world does someone who expects that have in mind? A world in which, whenever germs invade my body, God intervenes directly to ward off disease? A world in which I may grow old but never die? A world in which, when I hurt someone's feelings, God makes them feel better? A world in which the stove suddenly goes off when a young child reaches for the burner? A world in which people who have wasted their money for years get a windfall because they earnestly prayed for a way to send their children to college? A world in which, when I pray for a hurricane not to strike where I live, it turns aside and strikes where you live? A world in which, when I'm worn out and need some sleep, God sees to it that the sun doesn't rise for a few extra hours?

And what if you were praying for a beautiful sunrise to enjoy early that morning?

You get my point. I don't know what kind of world this would be. I can't even imagine it. For it would be a world without any order or regularity. We could depend on nothing, since we'd never know when God would be cutting the cards again. I don't disbelieve in miracles, but, almost by definition, they have to be rare. Otherwise life becomes impossible.

What sounds pious and devout — that we should expect God to work a miracle in our life at any time — doesn't really take God seriously. He's not a magician at our beck and call. And the course of the world should not be rearranged every time we want things different. That notion is, if you think about it, the ultimate in narcissism — as if I were at the center of the universe. To take God seriously is to leave the center to him.

At least in most cases, this is, I think, the inner meaning of the miracles of Jesus in the Gospels. They are an announcement that God's presence has drawn near in Jesus, and that we are to turn to him. And remember, the people he heals eventually get sick again and die. And the great miracle — Easter — doesn't encourage us to expect God to perform miracles every day. It teaches us that the miracle of new life comes only on the other side of the cross and the grave.

Something else about this view of Jean's disturbs me even more. Whoever taught her to think this way has done her a great disservice. Now she thinks that if miracles aren't happening in her life, it must be because her faith is weak, or because she doesn't have the courage to pray with real confidence. Somebody said to her, "God will help you; expect God to help you if you ask him." When she doesn't see the help, she's likely to conclude that she lacks faith. So those words that were supposed to boost her faith turn out to undercut it. Remember: it isn't good news if it isn't heard as good news.

I don't mean that you shouldn't bring your needs and wants to God. Of course you should. Not because you expect him to satisfy every one of them, but simply because you want to share with him what's in the center of your life. But when you bring them, it's good to let Jesus be your model: "Not my will, but thine be done." That's the cure for narcissism.

Love,
Mom

Peace of Mind

Dear Ellen:

Why is it always wrong to go against conscience? I'm not surprised that you find the whole matter a little puzzling, but I think your professor is right about that. I'm not so certain about his reasons, though, at least as you report them to me.

Too often these days we think of conscience simply as an inner feeling, sincerely held. If that's what conscience is, then being sincere is pretty much the same as being right. And, of course, I can't deny that plenty of people seem to think sincerity is all that counts. You should remember, though, that very bad things have been done by people who were quite sincerely doing what they thought best.

Train yourself to think of conscience in a different way —not as an inner feeling but as a judgment. When you deliberate about a problem, you finally come to a point where your mind is made up. At that point you might say: "If I didn't do this, I would be going against my conscience." That conscience is simply the end product of your deliberation — your last and best judgment about what you should do.

Once we picture it that way, it's clear why we should never act contrary to our conscience. For that would be to embrace what you take to be evil. This way of thinking still leaves open the possibility that your conscience might be objectively wrong. Your last and best judgment might be a mistaken one. Subjectively, however, you of course won't think so. Hence, you can hardly act in any other way without willingly undertaking to do (what you think) evil. And that no one ought ever do.

So we can say both that your conscientious judgment might be objectively mistaken *and*, subjectively, that you must always act in accord with it. If I understand your questions rightly, though, I think I can tell you what's really bothering you.

A kind of gap opens up between what is actually right and what you might conscientiously believe should be done. You could deliberate in all sincerity, be obligated to act in accord with the judgment resulting from such conscientious reflection, and yet do what is morally wrong. There is something a little terrifying about that, isn't there?

Part of the tragedy of life is that equally conscientious people may sometimes find themselves locked in moral — even mortal — disagreement. One may in all sincerity, with a good conscience, do something terribly evil. That's what worries you, and I'm afraid I can only say that it is a genuine possibility. If evil always wore a sign identifying itself clearly for us, life would be a lot simpler than it is.

Remember the book that was so popular a few years back about why bad things happen to good people? I think the deeper problem is why (objectively) bad things are done by (subjectively) good people. One way to solve the problem, of course, is just to call "good" whatever is sincerely done. It sounds as if that's the direction your professor was moving. But I don't think that takes seriously enough the terrors of conscientious behavior.

At the end of the day, I don't think one should take much comfort in the fact that one's conscience is at rest. A peaceful conscience is not an infallible sign that I have done what is right. It may only indicate that my conscience has been deformed in certain ways, or that I have become expert at repressing truths I ought to see. What you need is not a peaceful conscience but what Helmut Thielicke once termed a comforted conscience.

You don't get that by turning inward and trying still harder to make sure you've been conscientious. You get it by turning outside yourself to God's gracious acceptance. You genuinely are what he says you are. Trust that — and don't look for peace of mind elsewhere.

Love,
Mom

Doing One's Best

Dear Ellen:

I'll say this for Professor Remchine: He's getting you to think about some hard and important questions. Can I do something wrong, know it is wrong, do it intentionally, and still have faith in God — the faith that makes me, even in that moment of doing wrong, a forgiven sinner?

The first thing to say, of course, is that faith involves the mysteriously hidden center of a person. Because it does, only God knows its presence or absence. I can't make that determination about anyone else — or even about myself. Only God sees us whole and entire, as we truly are.

So all we can do is say what is possible, not what is actual. But let's take the case you proposed. Brent has a research paper due. He's done a good bit of reading and thinking about the topic but hasn't gotten the paper written. He must pass this class to graduate, and so he borrows a paper his sister had written a few years earlier, revises it slightly, and turns it in. He knows this is wrong yet he can't bring himself to do otherwise. Taking this class over again would mean more time and expense — both in short supply for him just now. He has, in fact, worked hard in the course, he's tired and anxious, he

55

has a job waiting for him after he graduates — this is the best he can manage.

Now you want to know what we should say about Brent. Can he have faith while deliberately sinning? A nice problem, if I may put it that way.

Be clear about one thing, though. We're not asking whether what he does is right. As I understand the case, we're all agreed that his action is wrong, and I don't think it would be too hard to give some reasons why it is. What you want to know is whether the *person* who deliberately does this wrong *act* can nonetheless be right with God — whether that is possible, leaving the actual state of Brent's relation to God as God's own secret.

Respondeo (as Aquinas would have said): Yes, I think it quite possible in such circumstances for Brent to have faith — the saving faith that trusts God's promise and therefore covers the sinner entirely with Christ's righteousness. Here's the question that is, I think, at the heart of your problem: Is Brent really embracing evil *as evil*? And, of course, he might be — in which case he could not simultaneously be asking God to be with him. But I suspect that Brent may be saying something like, "I know it's wrong, but this is *the best* I can manage right now."

That is, he embraces his admittedly wrong action not as evil but as a good — as the best he can manage. You may, of course, say with some justification: "If he seriously asks God for help, God would enable him to do what is right." Maybe so. But who are we to say what God must do for Brent? It seems, in fact, that he has not given Brent the strength to make such a decision now. The one thing we *can* say is that in Jesus God has demonstrated decisively that he accepts sinners. Brent should trust that as a sinner he, too, is accepted.

Brent certainly does not yet have within himself the stuff that makes a martyr. And he needs to realize that — in a way hard to specify — what we *do* will gradually shape who we *are*. He can slowly become a person unable — and finally unwilling — to trust God to care for him. But, in a distorted and deficient way, he does still cling to what is good. He does the best he can manage. Clinging to the good, even in so distorted a way, he clings ultimately to God. And that, I think, is faith.

Look sometime at the story of Naaman and Elisha in 2 Kings. After being healed, Naaman prepares to return to Syria where he is a commander in the army. He takes back with him a little Israelite soil in order, even in Syria, to worship Israel's God. But he adds: "'In this matter may the Lord pardon your servant: when my master goes into the house of Rimmon to worship there, leaning on my arm, and I bow myself in the house of Rimmon, when I bow myself in the house of Rimmon, the Lord pardon your servant in this matter.' Elisha said to him, 'Go in peace.'"

Love,
Mom

Passing Exams

Dear Ellen:

It sounds as if you've been busy doing many things. I hope, though, that you are keeping up with your work. Final exams are not that far away, you know, and I can tell you that it will be harder to take exams in the Spring than it was in the Fall.

The exams themselves aren't harder, of course, but preparing yourself psychologically for the effort is. There's something about the spring — the weather is getting nicer, you're coming to the end of a long year of hard work, there's always a temptation to quit just a little early. Whatever the reasons, I predict you'll find it's hard to concentrate your mind.

Before you write to remind me, I will acknowledge that Jesus said, "Take no thought for the morrow." Would that you took everything he said with the seriousness you have been taking that saying of late. Moreover, if you were to look at the whole verse, it might seem a bit more complicated. "Do not be anxious about tomorrow, for tomorrow will be anxious for itself. Let the day's own trouble be sufficient for the day."

The question you must therefore ask is: What is *today's* trouble that requires my attention today, even if I am not anxious about tomorrow? And *today's* task, it turns out, is preparing yourself for what is to come on a succession of tomorrows. You are not to be anxious, not to live in fear of what is to come; for you commit that future to God's safekeeping. But precisely because you have been set free from such anxiety, you can apply yourself industriously to the tasks God sets before you today — like preparing for your exams.

That, at any rate, is what I think the passage means. When Jesus says, "don't worry," he doesn't mean that God will always provide what we need. He means that even if we lack some things we are still safe with God. Therefore, don't worry.

You know, Ellen, I probably wouldn't bother to write this to you if the point applied only to final exams. I'm confident you won't ignore your preparation for them. The more general point, though, is one that applies to the whole of your life. It won't be many years until you're thinking back with fond memories to your easy life as a student. For, in fact, life will get harder and more hectic, and there will be "exams" of many different sorts. You and your friends realize that, of course, even if the full reality hasn't yet sunk in. Maybe that's why so many students today seem burdened with anxiety about the future.

I know lots of people my age, in fact, who seem very anxious about the future even while they're looking for ways to cut back their working hours today. To me, at least, this seems to get it backwards. We should place our future into God's hands and then, free of worry about it, be energized for the tasks set before us in the present.

Easier to say than to do, of course. I know that. But there's a deep psychological truth that we don't always appreciate in the Christian faith. Remember when Paul first started going out with Janet — how he was always trying to figure out what she'd like to do best? No idea was ever quite good enough. That is to say, he was always a little anxious, a little worried that things wouldn't go well. And how in the world can things go well when you're that tied in knots?

Once he was confident that she really did care about him, he was set free. He didn't stop trying to please her, but he did it with a joy and confidence — even an energy — that hadn't been there before. All the energy that had gone into coping with anxiety was now liberated. Just so between us and God. He is pleased with you and will, one way or another, take care of you. That's the point of the story of Jesus. So the energy that might go into worry about the future can be set free — not to do simply as you please but to work hard at the tasks God sets before you this very day. For the moment, that probably means chemistry.

Love,
Mom

Summer Lessons

Dear Ellen:

Where did the summer go? And why do I say that every year when school starts again? I hope you're settled back into your routine by now; I'm beginning to get there.

Once you leave for college, it's never quite the same when you come home, is it? You've crossed a threshold in life and there's no turning back. That's good, of course. It's the way things should be. You have to grow up, and I, alas, have to grow old. (Or can we, at least for the moment, just say "older"?)

But accepting this as the truth of life, and accepting even that it is good, we can shed a tear for what you've left behind — for the beauty of a child's summers. What were your summer vacations but a recurring set of lessons — some of the most important lessons in life — that can be learned in few other ways?

You learned to care for nature — sun, trees, lakes, flowers, vegetables. You lived a little less artificially, a little less governed by the clock. You learned the lure of something — like a thunderstorm — that is beautiful and terrifying at the same time. (That's how Aslan is described in the Narnia stories. Do you remember?) And you learned, of course, that nature can be a beautiful garden only if it is weeded and cared for by disciplined labor. Its pleasures are never unmixed — there are mosquitoes, after all — and so it can only be an intimation of greater joy, not the completion of our heart's desire.

You had time to read — just lie on the couch and read *Pride and Prejudice,* as you did a few weeks ago. When you were little it was *The Bobbsey Twins,* and I bet you'll return to Bert and Nan, Freddie and Flossie, years from now just to evoke some of the imaginative pleasure of your childhood. More important, though, you had the chance to see the world through many eyes, reading all sorts of books — some serious, some pretty frivolous. I notice that kids David's age are bombarded at school with talk about the importance of diversity and "valuing" the experience of others. But it doesn't seem to be taking hold. By the time they enter college they're generally quite offended if anyone disagrees with them. Maybe we need to set them free just to read again.

Summer also gave you a chance to organize your own life a little, set your own schedule. (Though your father kept trying to organize it for you!) As you grow older you will see what a great gift that summertime leisure was, for you'll have precious few such opportunities in life. During the summer you can be a little quirky without having anything bad result. Children should be free in the summer — the better to be disciplined in school.

And without the summer . . . well, how could you have endured the school year? Is there any feeling quite like that one on the last day of school before summer vacation begins? It gives a dangerously giddy — and deceptive — sense of freedom. Deceptive, because so much of life won't be like that. Dangerous, because we can easily get into trouble when we start celebrating our freedom. But still, try to imagine life without that experience

— without knowing what it means to say, "The school term has ended." Without that, the whole school year would be a different experience. It would lose its sense of expectancy and we'd miss one of the ways most of us learn what it means to live in hope. Without that, we might start to think there could never be an end to the daily routine — and lose our taste for heaven.

I wouldn't say that the advocates of a longer school year are hostile toward either children or religion. But I worry about a world shaped by their concerns. I'm afraid such a world will be less open to the lessons summer taught you — which will make it a harder world for children, a more pedantic but perhaps less thoughtful world, and a world more likely to forget what it means to hope for heaven.

Love,
Mom

Turned Outward

Dear Ellen:

Your father and I loved reading about your own memories of summer. But we were also quite intrigued by the questions you raised about childhood. We decided that two quite opposite mistakes are being made today. We started with the obvious: many children are neglected and left pretty much to raise themselves. How many times when we picked you up after volleyball practice didn't we end up driving five or six other people home? They never seemed to have to be home at any particular time, never seemed to think that anyone might expect them. If we didn't drive them, they just hung around somewhere.

There's an opposite problem, though, and some of the comments in your letter set us to thinking about it. If some children are just set free, others are suffocated. In a kind of natural reaction to all those children left to raise themselves, some parents are too much with their children, have too much invested in them. They see their children as a replication of themselves in the world, a project by which they express themselves. There are times when even quite dedicated Christian parents fall into this trap. They forget that being a parent is a task, not an exercise in self-expression.

Such children get plenty of attention, but I worry about what they'll be like when they're a little older. It reminds me of a line I read in a novel not too long ago: "If from infancy you treat children as gods, they are liable in adulthood to act like devils." They have never learned to get along with different sorts of people. They're easily offended. They turn differences of opinion into major issues, losing all ability to distinguish genuinely important moral questions from their likes and dislikes. So we live in a world where you can't tell a joke that treads on ethnic sensibilities or refer to a disabled person as "handicapped," but you can abort a baby if it happens to have a genetic defect.

I'm not sure how we can make our way back to a saner understanding of parents, and children. Public schools are often totalitarian institutions, almost hostile toward parents' desires to have a hand in shaping their own children. In response, though, parents may want their children subject to no influence but their own — a poor recipe for raising a child, I think.

There is a fascinating passage in Thomas Aquinas about the incest taboo. If we could give an obvious explanation why some behavior is prohibited, we wouldn't experience it as taboo — only as wrong. Still, sometimes we may be able to discern a deeper meaning. When Aquinas tries to explain the reason for the incest taboo, he suggests that it is aimed at increasing friendship within the human race. By forcing us to see as possible sexual partners only those who are not closely related, the taboo turns families outward, keeps them open to new and different ways of life.

That's good for us biologically, but it's also good morally. It forces us constantly to distinguish between moral matters that really count — and about which we should not compromise — and the habits of mind we're used to. Your friend Jonathan gets under your skin when he seems a little insensitive — but he's also a good (and even wise) person, and you're the better for having known him.

Love,
Mom

Conversing

Dear Ellen:

I'm sorry your professor offended you by making a joke about short people, but why not just laugh? Clearly, she had no malice toward you or anyone else — and, to be honest, the joke was rather witty. Think how dull your class would be if she — and all the rest of you — had to calculate before every comment whether anyone present might be offended in any way. That would be the death of all good conversation.

It's true, of course, that no serious conversation can occur if we let nothing engage us deeply enough to be offended. Conversation — whether in your class or outside it — requires people who care about things, who can become passionate about an idea or an interest. Inability to work up such concern about anyone or anything is pretty close to being dead. It may even be a kind of spiritual death — something akin to what medieval thinkers meant by sloth.

But there will also be no conversation worthy of the name if you can't learn to distance yourself a little from your commitments and passions. If you treat every disagreement as an attack upon your person, no one will want to talk with you for very long. Think about what that sort of response implies. It suggests that there is no merit at all in what the other person says. It treats that person's view not as a position a reasonable person might hold, but simply as personal criticism.

I will tell you now — you are old enough, I think — that it's this sort of problem that causes your father to avoid your Aunt Suzanne. He'll come up with all sort of reasons not to see her. He'll find something that takes him out of the room whenever she's around. I don't entirely approve, of course — and I give him little lectures to that effect. But I also understand what's bothering him. She can't — or won't — just converse. Within only a few minutes her voice is rising, its tone more shrill, and woe betide your father if he disagrees. Every issue is personal. It's easier for him just to leave the room and not come back for a while.

Of course, I'd also get tired of talking with someone who held no views at all on important matters, who just saw every side of a question without bringing his mind to a point on anything. There's finally something a little frivolous about such a person — as if the whole of life were play. And it's not.

But you can lighten up a little. Don't feel you must be on guard at every moment lest something offensive be said. Do your best to get inside the heads of your conversation partners and see how the issue looks from there. You will, in effect, be training yourself in the virtue of justice — trying to make the other person's case as strong as you can before responding to its weaknesses. That is the Golden Rule of conversation because it's the Golden Rule of life.

Nothing I've written means that you can't know your own mind on a matter. But that mind will be enlarged and enriched — and, not surprisingly, you will become a better conversation partner — if you have learned to think the other person's thoughts as clearly as you can. That, at any rate, is what I think. And rest assured — you're free to disagree.

Love,
Mom

Bending the Knee

Dear Ellen:

Thanks for sending me the flyer your congregation there uses to try to attract college students to its services. I wish I had found it more encouraging, though.

That line at the top of the flyer — "Sometimes questioning our answers is more important than answering our questions" — immediately reminded me of Pastor Moeller, who was Pastor Haden's predecessor. I suppose you were too young then to remember much of him, but this is exactly the sort of thing he would have said. I didn't find it very appealing then, and I don't now.

You will point out to me, of course, the importance of humility and the danger of dogmatism. That's an important reminder, and we need to take it seriously. But we also need to think carefully about what true humility is. To my ear, it's the statement on the flyer that sounds proud and narrow-minded.

If you would only take the course in modern religious thought that I've been recommending, you might be surprised to discover that the statement has a distinguished intellectual pedigree. It's not terribly different from a famous passage in the works of Lessing, a great figure of the German Enlightenment.

Lessing suggests that if God were to offer us in one hand the complete truth, and with the other hand offer the unending search for truth, we should choose the latter. We should choose it even if it meant we would always be in error. The journey is everything; arrival nothing.

But to hope that you might actually learn the truth about God is not pride. It is true humility — a humility that would be willing to bend the knee and adore. Bending the knee requires a kind of submission of self that continuing the quest for truth does not. And you'll find that those eternal questers are sometimes rather dogmatic. They live within a frame of reference that simply will not reckon with the possibility that their chatter must one day cease.

I have, for example, never known a less humble or more dogmatic person than Pastor Moeller. He was absolutely firm in his conviction that questions must remain open and unanswered. As a result, it was quite impossible ever to have a serious, pointed discussion with him. He thought he was open to all opinions, but, in fact, he never took seriously the views of many of his parishioners. On this point I am with Chesterton: "The purpose of opening the mind, as of opening the mouth, is to close it on something solid."

Of course, we are limited, imperfect creatures, and, hence, the form of our knowledge must be correspondingly limited. Such a realization is fine, as long as with all our heart we really desire to know the truth. But when we fall in love with an image of ourselves as fearless (and, of course, humble) seekers after truth, we often lose the sense that submission will one day be asked of us. That a powerful hand will take us by the shoulder, and an authoritative voice will tell us that the day has come to look and see. We do not finally set the terms for that encounter, and it can be dangerous to seek unless we truly desire to find.

When that day comes, we will certainly see how often we have been mistaken. Those intellectual mistakes will be covered with the same wide mercy that covers our moral failings. In fact, we will realize then how closely intertwined our moral and intellectual weaknesses have been — how often we were unable to relinquish the truth as we wanted it to be for the sake of the truth as it was, how often we engaged in self-assertion under the guise of submission. But all that will matter little because we will be where we desire to be — at journey's end, bathed in the light of the truth.

Our hearts are restless, St. Augustine said, until they rest in God. To suppose the journey more desirable than the homecoming is to begin to cut off desire. Eventually, then, even the journey will seem less serious a matter. The only humility you should seek is the humility proper to a creature not yet at home with her Creator. You must want that homecoming. To lose the capacity for adoration is to lose the humility that acknowledges our humanity — and, in acknowledging it, preserves it.

Love,
Mom

Giving Death a Hearing

Dear Ellen:

You're quite right about Mr. Leiter. He's a changed man since his brother died. Whether for better or worse is a hard question to answer, though. I would think I'd know someone pretty well after having lived next door to him all these years, but I admit that he has surprised me.

I can understand that you found it funny to see a 70-year-old man doing his "power walking" so faithfully. I have to smile sometimes, though I try to remember that things may look rather different to me 20 years from now. But to tell the truth, you don't know half the story of how he's changed his life. I've had several conversations with him about it when we were out in the yard. He eats nothing but bran for breakfast, has eliminated all red meat from his diet, allows himself a small scoop of ice cream once a week on Sunday, and is popping enough vitamins to keep the pharmacy in business all by himself.

I'm not quite sure how I feel about all this. Certainly it's hard to argue that we should not take care of our health. But it just seems so self-preoccupied. If he said, "I want to live long enough to see my grandchildren grow up a little," I'd be sympathetic. If he said, "I just don't think my wife would handle it very well if I died first," I'd be sympathetic. If he said, "You know, I'm not as energetic as I once was, but every time I watch the sun rise, the sheer beauty of it brings joy to my heart," I'd be sympathetic. If he even said, "I find that I still enjoy a good round of golf," I'd be moderately sympathetic.

But mainly he seems just to be saying, "I don't want to die." In which case, of course, he's in for a disappointment. Over the summer I read Reynolds Price's memoir of his battle with spinal cord cancer. It's a remarkable story and a remarkable book, but it also left me feeling somewhat divided. I don't think — though, of course, I don't know for sure — that I'd want to endure what he has just to stay alive. Yet his advice is: "Never give death a serious hearing till its ripeness forces your final attention and dignified nod."

That's very powerful. And when he says that, though a paraplegic, he writes "with the arm of a grateful man," I confess to being moved. But does that say everything that needs saying? To be sure, he's a step ahead of where Mr. Leiter seems to be, since he is at least prepared to give death that dignified nod when it leaves him little choice. Sooner or later, though, we all die of something. And there comes a point in life, I think, where one might well ask: "What is it that I want to die of?" If I keep stuffing down this bran every morning and getting in my three miles of power walking, if I keep my cardiovascular system robust, what sort of death will one day be mine? And will any of my friends be around to visit me in the nursing home?

What all of us secretly hanker for today is control of our dying. We want to keep it at bay for as long as possible — hence our obsessive concern with health, diet, fitness. But then, if it must come, we want it entirely on our own terms. That desire for control lies behind the current fascination with euthanasia. And, in a peculiar sort of way, Mr. Leiter's intense concern to stay alive and vigorous is closely related. He wants to be in control all the way. He doesn't want to wither or grow feeble. Certainly he doesn't want to suffer. But if one day that can't be avoided, what will he want then?

I will admit, before you write back to tell me, that it's easy to think about these matters when we're well and happy. True enough. But isn't that just the point? Now *is* the time to think about dying so that when the time comes we have a sense of who we are and how we ought to live in the face of death. Maybe when the time comes I'll decide that my earlier thoughts were mistaken. But maybe those settled ways of thinking will give me something strong and firm to grab and hold when I most need it.

Love,
Mom

Clinging and Falling

Dear Ellen:

No, I don't mind at all that you let Amy read these letters. But what does she mean saying that no mother would write letters like these to her daughter anymore? Tell her that I don't know whether to feel insulted or complimented.

I know what she means. As you said, she likes her letters a little more gossipy — what you did last Friday night, how the weekend's shaping up, and so forth. But we do plenty of that gossiping on the telephone, for which I have bills as proof.

Nor, I have to admit, am I particularly interested in trying to relive my own college years through you. For one thing, they weren't all that happy until I met your father. And for another, I firmly believe that "for everything there is a season." That doesn't mean I won't be happy to come and visit you for a weekend, but let's make it one when there's a good concert, not a basketball game.

You can tell Amy that she raised a question I don't claim to be able to answer. Certainly I didn't want to suggest that I feel particularly brave or confident in the face of death. On the contrary, I've known quite a few people over the years who would put me to shame on that score. The fact is, though, that we wither and die. In the face of such a truth about life, we seem able only to adopt one of two attitudes: We may welcome it, or we may oppose it. I myself am looking for a third, slightly more complex stance.

Do you remember that wonderful little chapter in *Bambi* in which no one appears except the two dried leaves still clinging to the oak tree long after the others had fallen?

> They were silent for a while. Then the first leaf said quietly to herself,
> "Why must we fall? . . ."
> The second leaf asked,
> "What happens to us when we have fallen?"
> "We sink down . . ."
> "What is under us?"
> The first leaf answered,
> "I don't know, some say one thing, some another, but nobody knows."
> The second leaf asked,
> "Do we feel anything, do we know anything about ourselves when we're down there?"
> The first leaf answered,
> "Who knows? Not one of all those down there has ever come back to tell us about it."

I think those lines take us about as far as human reason can manage. And as we read on in the chapter, we find that one of the leaves has learned to welcome life as it is, while the other has not. Each sees part of the truth, each has a certain dignity.

But you and I believe that one of those who fell down has come back to tell us about it. Tell us what? Not that there's nothing to fear, not that we should simply welcome death. Not, however, that we should simply oppose it forever, since he did not, and we follow after him. Maybe Reynolds Price's phrase wasn't too bad: When the time has clearly come, we will give death a "dignified nod." It's a great evil, but we trust that God can make something good of it — for us, as for Jesus. That takes us a little farther than the leaves could see.

> "Let's remember how beautiful it was, how wonderful, when the sun came out and shone so warmly that we thought we'd burst with life. Do you remember? And the morning dew, and the mild and splendid nights. . . ."
>
> A moist wind blew, cold and hostile, through the tree-tops.
>
> "Ah, now," said the second leaf. "I . . ." Then her voice broke off.
>
> She was torn from her place and spun down.
>
> Winter had come.

Some magnificent beauties, then the coming of that cold and hostile wind. Apart from Jesus, I think that's pretty much the truth of life.

Love,
Mom

Good Things

Dear Ellen:

So you thought that two successive letters about death was a bit much? Maybe so. But to begin to learn how to die is also to learn how to live as one who is not captive to every passing trend. In your case that may mean: not captive to whatever the current fashion in clothing may be.

You admit to being jealous of all the nice clothes Carrie has, especially since — as you so straightforwardly put it — we have just as much money as her parents do. True enough, I imagine, but that doesn't mean you shouldn't begin to discipline your desire for nice things.

Obviously, the desire isn't wrong in itself. If the things are good, then they're worth desiring. But in the scale of good things they don't rank quite as high as you suppose. To have some nice things to wear is desirable, and there's no good reason deliberately to dress down outlandishly as some college students do. But remember that your heart will be where your treasure is (though, as long as your father has anything to say about it, I don't think our treasure is going to be where your heart is).

I'll grant that wanting more (and more) clothes seems relatively innocent, but is it really? For one thing, you may become cruel without realizing it. Remember how when your father wears shorts you mock him because his socks come up too high. Of course, the jokes don't bother him; in fact, he probably pulls the socks a little higher whenever you're around. Pretty soon, though, you can find yourself judging people by whether they meet your exalted standard of dress. You may miss out on some good friends that way, and you may hurt some feelings. Are you sure that some fellow with his socks pulled up can't make a good husband?

Learning to discipline such desires will also prepare you for the years ahead. There's no guarantee that you'll have as much money for clothing as you suppose you will, nor do you want to let such desires be determinative in the choices you make. Do you just want the job that pays the most? Or the one that seems most worthwhile? Suppose you have a child who turns out to have special needs that draw heavily on your resources. Don't you want to become the sort of person who can do without some things, even some nice things that you'd really like to have? Simplicity makes possible generosity.

Of course, for someone else, like your father, clothes would constitute no temptation. With him we'd have to start talking about tools — how many he needs, how good they have to be. But the principle is the same. While enjoying the good things of life and taking pleasure in them as gifts from God, we need to learn not to rest our heart entirely in them. And it's hard to learn that lesson, I think, unless there's been a little renunciation in our life. For you it would be no great trick to say, "I guess I'll do without a new saw." But a new sweater — doing without it would be harder, and for you more worthwhile.

Most of us aren't often really tempted to steal. Many of us aren't even tempted to try to enrich ourselves unjustly at others' expense. So if such vices were all the commandment against stealing prohibited, it wouldn't reach very far into your life or mine. I suspect, though, that the commandment exists, at least in part, to help all of us learn to think about possessions — to remember that the "things" in our life will reach inside us and shape our inner spirit.

This doesn't mean you should start criticizing your friends when they have nice clothes. Simplicity and generosity can be learned in different ways by different people. And, of course, there is no virtue in supposing that everyone must do without what you do without. Chesterton had it right: "There is more simplicity in the man who eats caviar on impulse than in the man who eats grape-nuts on principle."

Love,
Mom

Getting a Life

Dear Ellen:

I've been meaning to say just a word about the broadest of topics
— your vocation in life. Maybe I should just say — about how
to "get a life."

What started me thinking about this was an incident at
church last week. They had a little dispute about who should
read the Scripture lessons at Sunday services. It seems that some
people want a chance to do it more often, while others are tired
of hearing them read poorly. Pastor Haden, a true child of his
time in matters liturgical, generally sides with the first group.
Says he is just a minister to equip ministers. (I sometimes think
the man was born uttering platitudes.)

Although I don't make an issue of it, I myself never read
the lessons. It's a form of silent witness — maybe even protest.
We have gradually begun to think of our "ministry" as doing
things at church and, especially, in a church service. This, in fact,
is what the liturgical renewal of the last few decades has largely
amounted to. It is a revival of exactly what the Reformers turned
away from in the 16th century — namely, the notion that only
certain vocations are religious.

For my part, I think of my vocation as the tasks I take up

daily — making and caring for home and family, teaching, being a (slightly apathetic but, I hope, dutiful) citizen. The difficulties and failures of that calling drive me back to the church's worship. The joys and beauties of the calling send me back to praise God. But the idea that the central expression of my faith might be reading the lessons . . . well, no thanks.

Once we start to think like that, we all have essentially the same vocation. And then, I guess, we may argue about who gets to do it this Sunday. How much better if we keep in mind that the one body has many members, with different gifts and callings.

I think of the fairy tale you used to like about the six servants. Remember how it went? The prince wanted to marry the beautiful princess, but her wicked mother would only give her hand in marriage to a suitor who could perform a series of difficult tasks. All the suitors had failed until the prince came along with his six unusual servants. The fat man who ate 300 oxen and drank 300 casks of wine overnight. The listener who could hear the princess crying far away where the queen had hidden her. Or the man who shivered when it got hot and burned when it got cold — and who sat in place of the prince on a huge bonfire for three days and nights and then said, "If it had lasted any longer, I might have frozen to death." You always loved that line. Usually we had to repeat it several times.

I think about this tale whenever the subject is vocation. The tall man didn't try to eat the 300 oxen. It was the listener, not the man with the long neck and good eyes, who listened for the princess crying. And the fat man didn't try to sit in the fire. Each did what he was asked to do and enabled to do, and the prince married his bride.

I think about this especially when I know someone who is suffering a lot, and I'm reminded how unequally suffering is distributed. Some people seem to face one problem after another, while others just roll along smoothly in life. There's no solving the "problem" of evil as a philosophical question, but we "live" this problem in the church when we remember that some bear more suffering than others because God calls them to that task. There's no more point to saying it isn't fair than there would be to claim it was unfair that only the fat man got to eat the 300 oxen. And, of course, if it's suffering we're talking about, remember that God plays by his own rules: He bears it for others.

Don't spend a lot of time worrying about what your calling may be. It will find you. Sometimes it will find you in the form of undeniable duty, even if the duty is one that you would like to set aside. Other times — probably most of the time — it will find you because you have certain talents and interests. Let them be your guide unless duty clearly says no.

When your calling brings joy, go to church and praise God for it. When you fail in your calling, go to church and hear the word of forgiveness. When your calling brings suffering, go to church and sit beneath the cross. And if your calling today should be to write a letter home, we will be glad to receive it.

Love,
Mom